This Journal Belongs to:

Email us at FREEBIES@JUNELUCY.COM
to get a FREE printable download!

FOR A LITTLE INSPIRATION
follow along at:

@JUNEANDLUCY

@JUNEANDLUCY

WWW.JUNELUCY.COM

Shop our other books at
www.junelucy.com

For questions and customer service, email us at
support@junelucy.com

Dreams are the small sprouts from which a brilliant tomorrow grows.

Dream Journaling: the Basics

When your head hits your soft pillow after a long day, you settle in for a rejuvenating night of restful slumber. However, while your body rests, your mind remains alive and you experience up to six dreams each night. Humans experience a vast array of dreams – from a stress dream about a looming work deadline to a fantasy vacation on a remote island paradise. Sometimes we experience hyper-realistic nightmares that result in waking up with a pounding heart and shortness of breath. The root cause of dreams remains unknown but scientists theorize that by dreaming, our brains are processing the millions of pieces of information we take in throughout the day. Some of this information is useless, and our brains dispose of it through our short-term memory. Sometimes our minds are working through a real-life problem and the solution appears in a dream state. And other times, a dream offers insight into complex emotions we may not even know we have. By writing down our dreams in a dream journal and looking at them critically, we can use dreams to our advantage and have fun during the process.

PROBLEM SOLVING AND MEMORY RETENTION

Have you ever had an "Aha!" moment in the middle of the night only to forget your dream a day later? You are not alone. It is estimated that up to 95% of our dreams are forgotten the next day. And this poses a problem when some of our best ideas and solutions come to us during the night. The Periodic Table of Elements, Mary Shelley's *Frankenstein*, and The Terminator were all created as the result of a dream. By documenting your dreams when you wake up, you are retaining valuable information and insight that you might otherwise forget. Use your dreams to spur creative artwork or solve a complicated issue you are struggling with.

FOSTER CREATIVITY

When we are in a creative slump, our minds still come alive at night. Use these inventive dreams as a springboard for daytime creativity. Turn your dream about a shadowy figure stalking you through a spooky house into a screenplay for the next big horror film. Or paint a picture of the enchanted forest with crystal blue pools that you visited in your dream. By tapping into these nighttime images, we are able to access an unending well of creativity.

PROCESS EMOTIONS

We have all had a dream where we oversleep for a big meeting or forget to show up to our child's dance recital. A lot of times our real life anxieties and fears manifest themselves in our dreams. The opposite can be true as well. We may have a dream about coconut drinks and the sand between our toes right before a highly anticipated trip to the beach. When we journal our dreams we can teach ourselves to identify and process emotions that we are holding deep down. The act of writing down the dreams along with our feelings, be it fear or joy, allows us to tap into our deep-rooted feelings and work toward resolutions.

LUCID DREAM

Would it surprise you to know that over half of all humans will experience a lucid dream during their life? This is the experience of being aware you are dreaming. As opposed to passively experiencing the dream, you comprehend the narrative and emotions of the dream and are sometimes able to control what happens next. There are a handful of methods people advocate in attempting to experience more frequent lucid dreams. For example, setting an alarm during the middle of the night and then returning to bed may trigger a lucid dream. But one practice many proponents of lucid dreaming frequently agree on is keeping a dream journal. By writing down your dreams, you are training your brain to become more aware of what occurs during your dream state. Thus you can practice becoming more and more aware that you are in a dream.

PINPOINT CONCRETE GOALS

We can also use our dream journal to help visualize and define goals. Use that dream about missing an important meeting to inspire an impressive PowerPoint presentation. Or turn that dream about winning the Olympics into a new practice schedule or exercise plan. Dreams can help identify what we value and desire. Turn those dreams into reality by setting goals and working toward them.

HOW TO USE THIS JOURNAL

This dream journal contains space for you to document and explore the dreams that come to you during the night. It is best to write down your dream as soon as you wake up while the memory is fresh, but you can journal any time of day (or night!). Include as much detail as you can remember. Small details may seem insignificant at first, but after time, you may notice patterns or recurring themes that you wouldn't have otherwise recognized. Track your sleep quality to give you additional insight – are you sleeping worse when you are stressed and does that present itself in your dreams? Label your dream with a title or theme to give it some context. Jot down any symbols that appear in your dream. And lastly, personalize and utilize this journal as you see fit. Have fun, get creative, and dream big!

Dream Symbols + Interpretations

There are certain dreams that seem to be almost universal to humankind. Whether suddenly falling, somehow ending up naked in an auditorium, or missing a big meeting, there are a handful of dreams that we've all had. Or maybe you have certain recurring symbols that show up frequently in your dreams, like a crystal clear lake or a slithery serpent. For years, people have tried to figure out why our brains concoct specific dreams at a given time. And while the science is still evolving, dream experts have identified some common dreams and what they could possibly mean to the dreamer.

Remember, these symbols are not one-size-fits-all. If the interpretation doesn't seem to fit, look at the dream from another angle. Sometimes dreams are just our brain's way of clearing space for the next day. But sometimes our dreams are more than they appear!

CHASED

The dream experts have two big theories about why you may be chased in your dream. One thought is that you have anxiety about something in your life that you may be avoiding. Or you may feel like something or someone is threatening your balance.

DEATH

While dreams about death might seem bleak, they are actually thought to be quite positive. If you dream about death or someone dying, it might mean a new beginning is on the horizon. Look to see if there are any exciting changes or opportunities ahead.

EXAM OR HOMEWORK

People often dream about missing a test or homework assignment long after they've graduated from school. Or perhaps you've moved on to dreaming about missing a big meeting or presentation. Sometimes we have these dreams because we're nervous about something. We're afraid to fail and feel unprepared.

FALLING

Dreams about falling are common and often end in waking with a sudden jolt. These dreams could indicate a loss of control or feeling insecure about some aspect of your life. People who experience lucid dreams report dreaming about falling quite often.

FLYING

If you dream you can fly, you are likely in a great place in life and have a feeling of control. People who dream about flying often report that they have a lot of good things going on in their real life.

LATE

If you dream you are late to something, whether it is an appointment or a dinner date, take a look inward and see if you need a life change. It could be something as small as reorganizing your closet or starting a new hobby. Or think bigger if you feel up for it!

NAKED

Another common dream is that you appear suddenly naked in public. Often the dreamer feels vulnerable in their real life. Maybe you have started a new relationship or job. These dreams can be either hopeful or daunting, depending on what you are feeling vulnerable about.

PREGNANCY

If you dream you are pregnant or had a baby, one theory is that you are experiencing growth and development in at least one area. Take a look at your professional, emotional, and personal life and try to see if you're experiencing growth in a specific place.

SNAKES

If you dream of a snake, you may need to take a look around and see if there is anyone or anything that is bringing toxicity into your life. Many dream analysts believe snakes can be a warning sign. But this is not always the case and sometimes a dream about a snake signifies growth and positive transformation.

TEETH

An odd dream frequently reported is that the dreamer loses their teeth. Interpretations are all over the map for this common dream. Maybe you are overwhelmed, concerned about your physical appearance, or are afraid of being embarrassed in some way.

WATER

Water can appear in different respects in a dream. Calm, serene waters reflect a sense of peace. Rising waters indicate feeling overwhelmed. A dirty puddle or mud may mean you are dwelling too much on the negative and need to come from a more positive mindset.

DATE: ____________ S M T W T F S

my sleep

SLEEP DURATION

SLEPT FROM ________ to ________ TOTAL SLEEP TIME ________ hrs ________ min

SLEEP QUALITY (CHECK ALL THAT APPLY)

☐ SOUND ☐ RESTLESS ☐ FREQUENT INTERRUPTIONS ☐ ____________

WHAT WOKE ME

☐ ALARM ☐ NATURALLY ☐ NOISE ☐ ____________

HOW I FELT UPON WAKING

☐ ENERGIZED ☐ REFRESHED ☐ TIRED ☐ GROGGY ☐ ____________

my dream

TITLE ______________________________

☐ FIRST TIME ☐ RECURRING ☐ SOME NEW, SOME RECURRING

DREAM SYMBOLS

description

____

____

____

____

____

____

____

____

____

____

____

interpretation + analysis

DATE: S M T W T F S *my sleep*

SLEEP DURATION

SLEPT FROM ________ to ________ TOTAL SLEEP TIME ________ hrs ________ min

SLEEP QUALITY (CHECK ALL THAT APPLY)

☐ SOUND ☐ RESTLESS ☐ FREQUENT INTERRUPTIONS ☐ ____________

WHAT WOKE ME

☐ ALARM ☐ NATURALLY ☐ NOISE ☐ ____________________________

HOW I FELT UPON WAKING

☐ ENERGIZED ☐ REFRESHED ☐ TIRED ☐ GROGGY ☐ ____________

my dream

TITLE ____

☐ FIRST TIME ☐ RECURRING ☐ SOME NEW, SOME RECURRING

DREAM SYMBOLS

description

interpretation + analysis

DATE: S M T W T F S

my sleep

SLEEP DURATION

SLEPT FROM _______ to _______ TOTAL SLEEP TIME _______ hrs _______ min

SLEEP QUALITY (CHECK ALL THAT APPLY)

☐ SOUND ☐ RESTLESS ☐ FREQUENT INTERRUPTIONS ☐ ___________

WHAT WOKE ME

☐ ALARM ☐ NATURALLY ☐ NOISE ☐ ___________

HOW I FELT UPON WAKING

☐ ENERGIZED ☐ REFRESHED ☐ TIRED ☐ GROGGY ☐ ___________

my dream

TITLE ___________

☐ FIRST TIME ☐ RECURRING ☐ SOME NEW, SOME RECURRING

DREAM SYMBOLS

description

interpretation + analysis

DATE: ____________ S M T W T F S

my sleep

SLEEP DURATION

SLEPT FROM ________ to ________ TOTAL SLEEP TIME ________ hrs ________ min

SLEEP QUALITY (CHECK ALL THAT APPLY)

☐ SOUND ☐ RESTLESS ☐ FREQUENT INTERRUPTIONS ☐ ____________

WHAT WOKE ME

☐ ALARM ☐ NATURALLY ☐ NOISE ☐ ____________

HOW I FELT UPON WAKING

☐ ENERGIZED ☐ REFRESHED ☐ TIRED ☐ GROGGY ☐ ____________

my dream

TITLE ____________________________

☐ FIRST TIME ☐ RECURRING ☐ SOME NEW, SOME RECURRING

DREAM SYMBOLS

description

interpretation + analysis

*Let the stars brighten
the path to your dreams.*

DATE: ____________ S M T W T F S

my sleep

SLEEP DURATION

SLEPT FROM ________ to ________ TOTAL SLEEP TIME ________ hrs ________ min

SLEEP QUALITY (CHECK ALL THAT APPLY)

☐ SOUND ☐ RESTLESS ☐ FREQUENT INTERRUPTIONS ☐ ____________

WHAT WOKE ME

☐ ALARM ☐ NATURALLY ☐ NOISE ☐ ____________

HOW I FELT UPON WAKING

☐ ENERGIZED ☐ REFRESHED ☐ TIRED ☐ GROGGY ☐ ____________

my dream

TITLE ____

☐ FIRST TIME ☐ RECURRING ☐ SOME NEW, SOME RECURRING

DREAM SYMBOLS

description

interpretation + analysis

DATE: ______________ S M T W T F S

my sleep

SLEEP DURATION

SLEPT FROM ________ to ________ TOTAL SLEEP TIME ________ hrs ________ min

SLEEP QUALITY (CHECK ALL THAT APPLY)

☐ SOUND ☐ RESTLESS ☐ FREQUENT INTERRUPTIONS ☐ ____________

WHAT WOKE ME

☐ ALARM ☐ NATURALLY ☐ NOISE ☐ ____________________________

HOW I FELT UPON WAKING

☐ ENERGIZED ☐ REFRESHED ☐ TIRED ☐ GROGGY ☐ ____________

my dream

TITLE ____

☐ FIRST TIME ☐ RECURRING ☐ SOME NEW, SOME RECURRING

DREAM SYMBOLS

description

interpretation + analysis

DATE: ____________ S M T W T F S

my sleep

SLEEP DURATION

SLEPT FROM ________ to ________ TOTAL SLEEP TIME ________ hrs ________ min

SLEEP QUALITY (CHECK ALL THAT APPLY)

☐ SOUND ☐ RESTLESS ☐ FREQUENT INTERRUPTIONS ☐ ____________

WHAT WOKE ME

☐ ALARM ☐ NATURALLY ☐ NOISE ☐ ____________________________

HOW I FELT UPON WAKING

☐ ENERGIZED ☐ REFRESHED ☐ TIRED ☐ GROGGY ☐ ____________

my dream

TITLE ____

☐ FIRST TIME ☐ RECURRING ☐ SOME NEW, SOME RECURRING

DREAM SYMBOLS

description

interpretation + analysis

DATE: ________ S M T W T F S

my sleep

SLEEP DURATION

SLEPT FROM ________ to ________ TOTAL SLEEP TIME ________ hrs ________ min

SLEEP QUALITY (CHECK ALL THAT APPLY)

☐ SOUND ☐ RESTLESS ☐ FREQUENT INTERRUPTIONS ☐ ____________

WHAT WOKE ME

☐ ALARM ☐ NATURALLY ☐ NOISE ☐ ____________

HOW I FELT UPON WAKING

☐ ENERGIZED ☐ REFRESHED ☐ TIRED ☐ GROGGY ☐ ____________

my dream

TITLE ____________

☐ FIRST TIME ☐ RECURRING ☐ SOME NEW, SOME RECURRING

DREAM SYMBOLS

description

interpretation + analysis

Dreams are today's creative solutions to tomorrow's problems.

DATE: ____________ S M T W T F S

my sleep

SLEEP DURATION

SLEPT FROM ________ to ________ TOTAL SLEEP TIME ________ hrs ________ min

SLEEP QUALITY (CHECK ALL THAT APPLY)

☐ SOUND ☐ RESTLESS ☐ FREQUENT INTERRUPTIONS ☐ ____________

WHAT WOKE ME

☐ ALARM ☐ NATURALLY ☐ NOISE ☐ ____________

HOW I FELT UPON WAKING

☐ ENERGIZED ☐ REFRESHED ☐ TIRED ☐ GROGGY ☐ ____________

my dream

TITLE ____

☐ FIRST TIME ☐ RECURRING ☐ SOME NEW, SOME RECURRING

DREAM SYMBOLS

description

interpretation + analysis

DATE: ______ S M T W T F S

my sleep

SLEEP DURATION

SLEPT FROM ________ to ________ TOTAL SLEEP TIME ________ hrs ________ min

SLEEP QUALITY (CHECK ALL THAT APPLY)

☐ SOUND ☐ RESTLESS ☐ FREQUENT INTERRUPTIONS ☐ ____________

WHAT WOKE ME

☐ ALARM ☐ NATURALLY ☐ NOISE ☐ ____________

HOW I FELT UPON WAKING

☐ ENERGIZED ☐ REFRESHED ☐ TIRED ☐ GROGGY ☐ ____________

my dream

TITLE ____________

☐ FIRST TIME ☐ RECURRING ☐ SOME NEW, SOME RECURRING

DREAM SYMBOLS

description

interpretation + analysis

DATE: ______ S M T W T F S

my sleep

SLEEP DURATION

SLEPT FROM ______ to ______ TOTAL SLEEP TIME ______ hrs ______ min

SLEEP QUALITY (CHECK ALL THAT APPLY)

☐ SOUND ☐ RESTLESS ☐ FREQUENT INTERRUPTIONS ☐ ______

WHAT WOKE ME

☐ ALARM ☐ NATURALLY ☐ NOISE ☐ ______

HOW I FELT UPON WAKING

☐ ENERGIZED ☐ REFRESHED ☐ TIRED ☐ GROGGY ☐ ______

my dream

TITLE ______

☐ FIRST TIME ☐ RECURRING ☐ SOME NEW, SOME RECURRING

DREAM SYMBOLS

description

interpretation + analysis

DATE: ____________ S M T W T F S

my sleep

SLEEP DURATION

SLEPT FROM ______ to ______ TOTAL SLEEP TIME ______ hrs ______ min

SLEEP QUALITY (CHECK ALL THAT APPLY)

☐ SOUND ☐ RESTLESS ☐ FREQUENT INTERRUPTIONS ☐ __________

WHAT WOKE ME

☐ ALARM ☐ NATURALLY ☐ NOISE ☐ __________

HOW I FELT UPON WAKING

☐ ENERGIZED ☐ REFRESHED ☐ TIRED ☐ GROGGY ☐ __________

my dream

TITLE __________

☐ FIRST TIME ☐ RECURRING ☐ SOME NEW, SOME RECURRING

DREAM SYMBOLS

description

interpretation + analysis

May you fall asleep with a peaceful mind and a dream in your heart.

DATE: ______________ S M T W T F S

my sleep

SLEEP DURATION

SLEPT FROM ________ to ________ TOTAL SLEEP TIME ________ hrs ________ min

SLEEP QUALITY (CHECK ALL THAT APPLY)

☐ SOUND ☐ RESTLESS ☐ FREQUENT INTERRUPTIONS ☐ ____________

WHAT WOKE ME

☐ ALARM ☐ NATURALLY ☐ NOISE ☐ ____________________________

HOW I FELT UPON WAKING

☐ ENERGIZED ☐ REFRESHED ☐ TIRED ☐ GROGGY ☐ ____________

my dream

TITLE ____

☐ FIRST TIME ☐ RECURRING ☐ SOME NEW, SOME RECURRING

DREAM SYMBOLS

description

interpretation + analysis

DATE: ________ S M T W T F S *my sleep*

SLEEP DURATION

SLEPT FROM ________ to ________ TOTAL SLEEP TIME ________ hrs ________ min

SLEEP QUALITY (CHECK ALL THAT APPLY)

☐ SOUND ☐ RESTLESS ☐ FREQUENT INTERRUPTIONS ☐ ____________

WHAT WOKE ME

☐ ALARM ☐ NATURALLY ☐ NOISE ☐ ____________________________

HOW I FELT UPON WAKING

☐ ENERGIZED ☐ REFRESHED ☐ TIRED ☐ GROGGY ☐ ____________

my dream

TITLE ____

☐ FIRST TIME ☐ RECURRING ☐ SOME NEW, SOME RECURRING

DREAM SYMBOLS

description

interpretation + analysis

DATE: ____________ S M T W T F S

my sleep

SLEEP DURATION

SLEPT FROM ________ to ________ TOTAL SLEEP TIME ________ hrs ________ min

SLEEP QUALITY (CHECK ALL THAT APPLY)

☐ SOUND ☐ RESTLESS ☐ FREQUENT INTERRUPTIONS ☐ ____________

WHAT WOKE ME

☐ ALARM ☐ NATURALLY ☐ NOISE ☐ ____________________

HOW I FELT UPON WAKING

☐ ENERGIZED ☐ REFRESHED ☐ TIRED ☐ GROGGY ☐ ____________

my dream

TITLE ____

☐ FIRST TIME ☐ RECURRING ☐ SOME NEW, SOME RECURRING

DREAM SYMBOLS

description

interpretation + analysis

DATE: ____________ S M T W T F S

my sleep

SLEEP DURATION

SLEPT FROM ________ to ________ TOTAL SLEEP TIME ________ hrs ________ min

SLEEP QUALITY (CHECK ALL THAT APPLY)

☐ SOUND ☐ RESTLESS ☐ FREQUENT INTERRUPTIONS ☐ ________

WHAT WOKE ME

☐ ALARM ☐ NATURALLY ☐ NOISE ☐ ________

HOW I FELT UPON WAKING

☐ ENERGIZED ☐ REFRESHED ☐ TIRED ☐ GROGGY ☐ ________

my dream

TITLE ________________

☐ FIRST TIME ☐ RECURRING ☐ SOME NEW, SOME RECURRING

DREAM SYMBOLS

description

interpretation + analysis

May your dreams be filled with magic that carries you through the night.

DATE: ______________ S M T W T F S

my sleep

SLEEP DURATION

SLEPT FROM ________ to ________ TOTAL SLEEP TIME ________ hrs ________ min

SLEEP QUALITY (CHECK ALL THAT APPLY)

☐ SOUND ☐ RESTLESS ☐ FREQUENT INTERRUPTIONS ☐ ____________

WHAT WOKE ME

☐ ALARM ☐ NATURALLY ☐ NOISE ☐ ____________

HOW I FELT UPON WAKING

☐ ENERGIZED ☐ REFRESHED ☐ TIRED ☐ GROGGY ☐ ____________

my dream

TITLE ____

☐ FIRST TIME ☐ RECURRING ☐ SOME NEW, SOME RECURRING

DREAM SYMBOLS

description

interpretation + analysis

DATE: ____________ S M T W T F S

my sleep

SLEEP DURATION

SLEPT FROM ________ to ________ TOTAL SLEEP TIME ________ hrs ________ min

SLEEP QUALITY (CHECK ALL THAT APPLY)

☐ SOUND ☐ RESTLESS ☐ FREQUENT INTERRUPTIONS ☐ ____________

WHAT WOKE ME

☐ ALARM ☐ NATURALLY ☐ NOISE ☐ ____________

HOW I FELT UPON WAKING

☐ ENERGIZED ☐ REFRESHED ☐ TIRED ☐ GROGGY ☐ ____________

my dream

TITLE ____________________________

☐ FIRST TIME ☐ RECURRING ☐ SOME NEW, SOME RECURRING

DREAM SYMBOLS

description

interpretation + analysis

DATE: ______ S M T W T F S

my sleep

SLEEP DURATION

SLEPT FROM ______ to ______ TOTAL SLEEP TIME ______ hrs ______ min

SLEEP QUALITY (CHECK ALL THAT APPLY)

☐ SOUND ☐ RESTLESS ☐ FREQUENT INTERRUPTIONS ☐ ______

WHAT WOKE ME

☐ ALARM ☐ NATURALLY ☐ NOISE ☐ ______

HOW I FELT UPON WAKING

☐ ENERGIZED ☐ REFRESHED ☐ TIRED ☐ GROGGY ☐ ______

my dream

TITLE ______

☐ FIRST TIME ☐ RECURRING ☐ SOME NEW, SOME RECURRING

DREAM SYMBOLS

description

interpretation + analysis

DATE: ____________ S M T W T F S

my sleep

SLEEP DURATION

SLEPT FROM _______ to _______ TOTAL SLEEP TIME _______ hrs _______ min

SLEEP QUALITY (CHECK ALL THAT APPLY)

☐ SOUND ☐ RESTLESS ☐ FREQUENT INTERRUPTIONS ☐ __________

WHAT WOKE ME

☐ ALARM ☐ NATURALLY ☐ NOISE ☐ __________

HOW I FELT UPON WAKING

☐ ENERGIZED ☐ REFRESHED ☐ TIRED ☐ GROGGY ☐ __________

my dream

TITLE ______________________________

☐ FIRST TIME ☐ RECURRING ☐ SOME NEW, SOME RECURRING

DREAM SYMBOLS

description

interpretation + analysis

The stars shine too bright to be afraid of the night.

DATE: ______ S M T W T F S *my sleep*

SLEEP DURATION

SLEPT FROM ______ to ______ TOTAL SLEEP TIME ______ hrs ______ min

SLEEP QUALITY (CHECK ALL THAT APPLY)

☐ SOUND ☐ RESTLESS ☐ FREQUENT INTERRUPTIONS ☐ ______

WHAT WOKE ME

☐ ALARM ☐ NATURALLY ☐ NOISE ☐ ______

HOW I FELT UPON WAKING

☐ ENERGIZED ☐ REFRESHED ☐ TIRED ☐ GROGGY ☐ ______

my dream

TITLE ______

☐ FIRST TIME ☐ RECURRING ☐ SOME NEW, SOME RECURRING

DREAM SYMBOLS

description

interpretation + analysis

DATE: ____________ S M T W T F S

my sleep

SLEEP DURATION

SLEPT FROM ________ to ________ TOTAL SLEEP TIME ________ hrs ________ min

SLEEP QUALITY (CHECK ALL THAT APPLY)

☐ SOUND ☐ RESTLESS ☐ FREQUENT INTERRUPTIONS ☐ ____________

WHAT WOKE ME

☐ ALARM ☐ NATURALLY ☐ NOISE ☐ ____________________________

HOW I FELT UPON WAKING

☐ ENERGIZED ☐ REFRESHED ☐ TIRED ☐ GROGGY ☐ ____________

my dream

TITLE ____

☐ FIRST TIME ☐ RECURRING ☐ SOME NEW, SOME RECURRING

DREAM SYMBOLS

description

interpretation + analysis

DATE: ____________ S M T W T F S

my sleep

SLEEP DURATION

SLEPT FROM ________ to ________ TOTAL SLEEP TIME ________ hrs ________ min

SLEEP QUALITY (CHECK ALL THAT APPLY)

☐ SOUND ☐ RESTLESS ☐ FREQUENT INTERRUPTIONS ☐ ____________

WHAT WOKE ME

☐ ALARM ☐ NATURALLY ☐ NOISE ☐ ____________________________

HOW I FELT UPON WAKING

☐ ENERGIZED ☐ REFRESHED ☐ TIRED ☐ GROGGY ☐ ____________

my dream

TITLE ____

☐ FIRST TIME ☐ RECURRING ☐ SOME NEW, SOME RECURRING

DREAM SYMBOLS

description

interpretation + analysis

DATE: ______ S M T W T F S

my sleep

SLEEP DURATION

SLEPT FROM ______ to ______ TOTAL SLEEP TIME ______ hrs ______ min

SLEEP QUALITY (CHECK ALL THAT APPLY)

☐ SOUND ☐ RESTLESS ☐ FREQUENT INTERRUPTIONS ☐ ______

WHAT WOKE ME

☐ ALARM ☐ NATURALLY ☐ NOISE ☐ ______

HOW I FELT UPON WAKING

☐ ENERGIZED ☐ REFRESHED ☐ TIRED ☐ GROGGY ☐ ______

my dream

TITLE ______

☐ FIRST TIME ☐ RECURRING ☐ SOME NEW, SOME RECURRING

DREAM SYMBOLS

description

interpretation + analysis

Dreams are lamp posts
guiding the midnight
highway of sleep.

DATE: ____________ S M T W T F S

my sleep

SLEEP DURATION

SLEPT FROM ________ to ________ TOTAL SLEEP TIME ________ hrs ________ min

SLEEP QUALITY (CHECK ALL THAT APPLY)

☐ SOUND ☐ RESTLESS ☐ FREQUENT INTERRUPTIONS ☐ ____________

WHAT WOKE ME

☐ ALARM ☐ NATURALLY ☐ NOISE ☐ ____________

HOW I FELT UPON WAKING

☐ ENERGIZED ☐ REFRESHED ☐ TIRED ☐ GROGGY ☐ ____________

my dream

TITLE ____

☐ FIRST TIME ☐ RECURRING ☐ SOME NEW, SOME RECURRING

DREAM SYMBOLS

description

interpretation + analysis

DATE: ____________ S M T W T F S

my sleep

SLEEP DURATION

SLEPT FROM ________ to ________ TOTAL SLEEP TIME ________ hrs ________ min

SLEEP QUALITY (CHECK ALL THAT APPLY)

☐ SOUND ☐ RESTLESS ☐ FREQUENT INTERRUPTIONS ☐ ____________

WHAT WOKE ME

☐ ALARM ☐ NATURALLY ☐ NOISE ☐ ____________

HOW I FELT UPON WAKING

☐ ENERGIZED ☐ REFRESHED ☐ TIRED ☐ GROGGY ☐ ____________

my dream

TITLE ____________

☐ FIRST TIME ☐ RECURRING ☐ SOME NEW, SOME RECURRING

DREAM SYMBOLS

description

interpretation + analysis

DATE: ____________ S M T W T F S

my sleep

SLEEP DURATION

SLEPT FROM ________ to ________ TOTAL SLEEP TIME ________ hrs ________ min

SLEEP QUALITY (CHECK ALL THAT APPLY)

☐ SOUND ☐ RESTLESS ☐ FREQUENT INTERRUPTIONS ☐ ____________

WHAT WOKE ME

☐ ALARM ☐ NATURALLY ☐ NOISE ☐ ____________________________

HOW I FELT UPON WAKING

☐ ENERGIZED ☐ REFRESHED ☐ TIRED ☐ GROGGY ☐ ____________

my dream

TITLE ____

☐ FIRST TIME ☐ RECURRING ☐ SOME NEW, SOME RECURRING

DREAM SYMBOLS

description

interpretation + analysis

DATE: ____________ S M T W T F S

my sleep

SLEEP DURATION

SLEPT FROM ________ to ________ TOTAL SLEEP TIME ________ hrs ________ min

SLEEP QUALITY (CHECK ALL THAT APPLY)

☐ SOUND ☐ RESTLESS ☐ FREQUENT INTERRUPTIONS ☐ ____________

WHAT WOKE ME

☐ ALARM ☐ NATURALLY ☐ NOISE ☐ ____________________________

HOW I FELT UPON WAKING

☐ ENERGIZED ☐ REFRESHED ☐ TIRED ☐ GROGGY ☐ ____________

my dream

TITLE ____

☐ FIRST TIME ☐ RECURRING ☐ SOME NEW, SOME RECURRING

DREAM SYMBOLS

description

interpretation + analysis

Dream lovely.
Sleep peacefully.
Wake joyfully.

DATE: ____________ S M T W T F S

my sleep

SLEEP DURATION

SLEPT FROM ________ to ________ TOTAL SLEEP TIME ________ hrs ________ min

SLEEP QUALITY (CHECK ALL THAT APPLY)

☐ SOUND ☐ RESTLESS ☐ FREQUENT INTERRUPTIONS ☐ ____________

WHAT WOKE ME

☐ ALARM ☐ NATURALLY ☐ NOISE ☐ ____________

HOW I FELT UPON WAKING

☐ ENERGIZED ☐ REFRESHED ☐ TIRED ☐ GROGGY ☐ ____________

my dream

TITLE ____________

☐ FIRST TIME ☐ RECURRING ☐ SOME NEW, SOME RECURRING

DREAM SYMBOLS

description

interpretation + analysis

DATE: ______ S M T W T F S *my sleep*

SLEEP DURATION

SLEPT FROM ______ to ______ TOTAL SLEEP TIME ______ hrs ______ min

SLEEP QUALITY (CHECK ALL THAT APPLY)

☐ SOUND ☐ RESTLESS ☐ FREQUENT INTERRUPTIONS ☐ ______

WHAT WOKE ME

☐ ALARM ☐ NATURALLY ☐ NOISE ☐ ______

HOW I FELT UPON WAKING

☐ ENERGIZED ☐ REFRESHED ☐ TIRED ☐ GROGGY ☐ ______

my dream

TITLE ______

☐ FIRST TIME ☐ RECURRING ☐ SOME NEW, SOME RECURRING

DREAM SYMBOLS

description

interpretation + analysis

DATE: ____________ S M T W T F S

my sleep

SLEEP DURATION

SLEPT FROM _______ to _______ TOTAL SLEEP TIME _______ hrs _______ min

SLEEP QUALITY (CHECK ALL THAT APPLY)

☐ SOUND ☐ RESTLESS ☐ FREQUENT INTERRUPTIONS ☐ ____________

WHAT WOKE ME

☐ ALARM ☐ NATURALLY ☐ NOISE ☐ ____________

HOW I FELT UPON WAKING

☐ ENERGIZED ☐ REFRESHED ☐ TIRED ☐ GROGGY ☐ ____________

my dream

TITLE ____________

☐ FIRST TIME ☐ RECURRING ☐ SOME NEW, SOME RECURRING

DREAM SYMBOLS

description

interpretation + analysis

DATE: ________ S M T W T F S

my sleep

SLEEP DURATION

SLEPT FROM ________ to ________ TOTAL SLEEP TIME ________ hrs ________ min

SLEEP QUALITY (CHECK ALL THAT APPLY)

☐ SOUND ☐ RESTLESS ☐ FREQUENT INTERRUPTIONS ☐ ____________

WHAT WOKE ME

☐ ALARM ☐ NATURALLY ☐ NOISE ☐ ____________________________

HOW I FELT UPON WAKING

☐ ENERGIZED ☐ REFRESHED ☐ TIRED ☐ GROGGY ☐ ____________

my dream

TITLE ____

☐ FIRST TIME ☐ RECURRING ☐ SOME NEW, SOME RECURRING

DREAM SYMBOLS

description

interpretation + analysis

Enjoy your adventure in the forest of dreams.

DATE: S M T W T F S

my sleep

SLEEP DURATION

SLEPT FROM _______ to _______ TOTAL SLEEP TIME _______ hrs _______ min

SLEEP QUALITY (CHECK ALL THAT APPLY)

☐ SOUND ☐ RESTLESS ☐ FREQUENT INTERRUPTIONS ☐ ___________

WHAT WOKE ME

☐ ALARM ☐ NATURALLY ☐ NOISE ☐ ___________

HOW I FELT UPON WAKING

☐ ENERGIZED ☐ REFRESHED ☐ TIRED ☐ GROGGY ☐ ___________

my dream

TITLE ___________

☐ FIRST TIME ☐ RECURRING ☐ SOME NEW, SOME RECURRING

DREAM SYMBOLS

description

interpretation + analysis

DATE: ________ S M T W T F S

my sleep

SLEEP DURATION

SLEPT FROM ______ to ______ TOTAL SLEEP TIME ______ hrs ______ min

SLEEP QUALITY (CHECK ALL THAT APPLY)

☐ SOUND ☐ RESTLESS ☐ FREQUENT INTERRUPTIONS ☐ __________

WHAT WOKE ME

☐ ALARM ☐ NATURALLY ☐ NOISE ☐ __________

HOW I FELT UPON WAKING

☐ ENERGIZED ☐ REFRESHED ☐ TIRED ☐ GROGGY ☐ __________

my dream

TITLE __________

☐ FIRST TIME ☐ RECURRING ☐ SOME NEW, SOME RECURRING

DREAM SYMBOLS

description

interpretation + analysis

DATE: ____________ S M T W T F S

my sleep

SLEEP DURATION

SLEPT FROM ________ to ________ TOTAL SLEEP TIME ________ hrs ________ min

SLEEP QUALITY (CHECK ALL THAT APPLY)

☐ SOUND ☐ RESTLESS ☐ FREQUENT INTERRUPTIONS ☐ ____________

WHAT WOKE ME

☐ ALARM ☐ NATURALLY ☐ NOISE ☐ ____________________________

HOW I FELT UPON WAKING

☐ ENERGIZED ☐ REFRESHED ☐ TIRED ☐ GROGGY ☐ ____________

my dream

TITLE ____

☐ FIRST TIME ☐ RECURRING ☐ SOME NEW, SOME RECURRING

DREAM SYMBOLS

description

interpretation + analysis

A night without dreams
is like a cupcake
without frosting.

DATE: ______ S M T W T F S

my sleep

SLEEP DURATION

SLEPT FROM ______ to ______ TOTAL SLEEP TIME ______ hrs ______ min

SLEEP QUALITY (CHECK ALL THAT APPLY)

☐ SOUND ☐ RESTLESS ☐ FREQUENT INTERRUPTIONS ☐ ______

WHAT WOKE ME

☐ ALARM ☐ NATURALLY ☐ NOISE ☐ ______

HOW I FELT UPON WAKING

☐ ENERGIZED ☐ REFRESHED ☐ TIRED ☐ GROGGY ☐ ______

my dream

TITLE ______

☐ FIRST TIME ☐ RECURRING ☐ SOME NEW, SOME RECURRING

DREAM SYMBOLS

description

interpretation + analysis

DATE: ______ S M T W T F S

my sleep

SLEEP DURATION

SLEPT FROM ______ to ______ TOTAL SLEEP TIME ______ hrs ______ min

SLEEP QUALITY (CHECK ALL THAT APPLY)

☐ SOUND ☐ RESTLESS ☐ FREQUENT INTERRUPTIONS ☐ ______

WHAT WOKE ME

☐ ALARM ☐ NATURALLY ☐ NOISE ☐ ______

HOW I FELT UPON WAKING

☐ ENERGIZED ☐ REFRESHED ☐ TIRED ☐ GROGGY ☐ ______

my dream

TITLE ______

☐ FIRST TIME ☐ RECURRING ☐ SOME NEW, SOME RECURRING

DREAM SYMBOLS

description

interpretation + analysis

DATE: ______ S M T W T F S

my sleep

SLEEP DURATION

SLEPT FROM ______ to ______ TOTAL SLEEP TIME ______ hrs ______ min

SLEEP QUALITY (CHECK ALL THAT APPLY)

☐ SOUND ☐ RESTLESS ☐ FREQUENT INTERRUPTIONS ☐ ______

WHAT WOKE ME

☐ ALARM ☐ NATURALLY ☐ NOISE ☐ ______

HOW I FELT UPON WAKING

☐ ENERGIZED ☐ REFRESHED ☐ TIRED ☐ GROGGY ☐ ______

my dream

TITLE ______

☐ FIRST TIME ☐ RECURRING ☐ SOME NEW, SOME RECURRING

DREAM SYMBOLS

description

interpretation + analysis

Sleep. Dream. Repeat.

DATE: ______ S M T W T F S

my sleep

SLEEP DURATION

SLEPT FROM ______ to ______ TOTAL SLEEP TIME ______ hrs ______ min

SLEEP QUALITY (CHECK ALL THAT APPLY)

☐ SOUND ☐ RESTLESS ☐ FREQUENT INTERRUPTIONS ☐ ______

WHAT WOKE ME

☐ ALARM ☐ NATURALLY ☐ NOISE ☐ ______

HOW I FELT UPON WAKING

☐ ENERGIZED ☐ REFRESHED ☐ TIRED ☐ GROGGY ☐ ______

my dream

TITLE ______

☐ FIRST TIME ☐ RECURRING ☐ SOME NEW, SOME RECURRING

DREAM SYMBOLS

description

interpretation + analysis

DATE: ______________ S M T W T F S

my sleep

SLEEP DURATION

SLEPT FROM _______ to _______ TOTAL SLEEP TIME _______ hrs _______ min

SLEEP QUALITY (CHECK ALL THAT APPLY)

☐ SOUND ☐ RESTLESS ☐ FREQUENT INTERRUPTIONS ☐ ____________

WHAT WOKE ME

☐ ALARM ☐ NATURALLY ☐ NOISE ☐ ____________________________

HOW I FELT UPON WAKING

☐ ENERGIZED ☐ REFRESHED ☐ TIRED ☐ GROGGY ☐ ____________

my dream

TITLE ____

☐ FIRST TIME ☐ RECURRING ☐ SOME NEW, SOME RECURRING

DREAM SYMBOLS

description

interpretation + analysis

Made in the USA
Middletown, DE
16 December 2021

56021500R00064